My Baby You'll Be

Sarah Fultz Adams

To the child we never got to meet,
but whom we will always love

Reminder

—

There will never be a neutral view on motherhood,
Besides respect.

Someone will always
Read too far into it,
Be triggered,
Feel attacked,
Express agreement,
Want to change –
And that's okay.

Our individual experiences,
Relationships,
Environments
And values
Mix together with our
Unique thoughts, emotions, feelings.

We crave connection,
Approval and
Acceptance.
We simply want to relate to other people.

Motherhood is a tricky one –
No desire to be a mom,
Trying for years to be a mom,
Pregnant,
One kid,
Two kids,
Fur kids,
Feathered kids,
Adopted kids,
Blended families,
The list goes on and on.

And it's beautiful.

Her story is beautiful.
Your story is beautiful.

It's okay to be different,
But it's important to respect that difference.

It's important to think of your infertile-but-fighting-so-hard friend
When inviting her to a birthday party
With 30 one-year-olds.

It's important to consider your single mom friend
When planning a last-minute girls' night
On a Tuesday.

Check in with your friends,
Your family,
Yourself.

Be kind.
Be considerate.
Be uplifting.
Be gentle.
Be respectful.

—
Every now and then,
I get a teensy glimpse into what
Motherhood might be like.

Hershey follows me into every room,
Needing to be picked up and held constantly.

Apollo gets sick and needs
All my attention,
Cuddles,
And belly rubs.

Lucky starts scratching at her ears,
And needs me to clean them.

Lagertha needs more attention,
Even though she got a hug five minutes ago.
She runs over and empties the toy box
Again
To make her point.

I separate two puppies
Who are quarreling
Over the same toy.
I take the toy away.

It might not look the same
As your motherhood,
But it's mine.

—
Smile and nod,
Smile and nod.

I kept my smiley mask on
For the doctor who was
Telling us –
And illustrating with
Lines and figures drawn upside down, facing us –
That we were looking at
A little less than a 5% chance.
Maybe 3-ish.
A 3-ish percent chance.

Beside me, my husband was nodding too.

We knew it wasn't going to be awesome news.
But hey –
He wasn't saying zero!

—

I bought a minivan
When I turned 23.

I'm not sure why
They were so appealing to me,
But I wanted one.

So much space, storage, and safety.
So comfortable.
So – family-oriented?

We got a lot of weird looks
When we showed off the minivan.
Long pauses.
"Um, is there something you want to tell us?"
"Are you pregnant?"
"Why?"

Even back then,
We were trying to get to you.

Strained smiles,
"No. I just wanted one."

—
When we got our first puppy together,
We were smitten.
I had picked out her name –
Hershey –
Before we officially met her.
She was teensy,
And spent her first few months
Riding around in David's sweatshirt hood
Or chasing after toys.

Soon, we found Apollo.
Goofy, happy and gorgeous
Apollo – who David got to name.

We had our two pups
And we were happy,
But life had other plans.

> Didn't you want a big family?
> You did say you're trying to grow your family, yes?
>
> ...Oh, with human children?
> Honestly you didn't technically specify.

Lucky came into our lives a couple years later –
Seeking shelter from who knows
What kind of abuse.
She slowly warmed up to us,
And added a wise, leisurely energy
We didn't know we were missing.

About a year and a half later,
Lagertha found David.
A sweet puppy
Full of energy –

Our little spaz.
She wanted attention, but was terrified
Of anyone who went near her.
Lagertha took a bit longer to trust her
New family,
But she was the most perfect
(and hopefully the last for now – ha)
addition to our pack.

God works in mysterious ways.
　　　This is what you've been praying for, my love.

—
Before taking any tests,
I started planning for you –
Imagining life with you.

I thought about
What schools we were near,
What house we were in,
What would take your interest.

Would you be super social and outgoing like your dad?
Would you want to stay in like your mom?
Would you have 4 shadows, following you everywhere?

I dreamed about
What your favorite color would be,
What types of books you'd like to read,
What your laughter would sound like.

—
I knew you were here.

I felt different –
More full, whole.

I felt an inexplicable need to move
More carefully,
Slower,
With more purpose.

I felt a
Nervousness
That I couldn't place.

I avoided buying a test,
Because I thought I knew already,
And I loved the
Privacy
Intimacy
Secret
Of having you all to myself.

Telling your dad, though, made it even better.

—
I took four pregnancy tests
Over a three-day timespan
Just to be sure
Before I told your dad.

I'd always imagined doing
Something elaborate
And sweet,
With a photographer present
And photos to cherish.

But in that moment –
When I decided I was sure –
I couldn't bear to go
One more second
Without your dad knowing,
Without him experiencing this joy with me.

I stumbled through it,
Trying not to cry all the
Happy tears,
And let him take it in.

He was so happy.

———

You are love.
You are happiness.
You are excitement.
You are mesmerizing.
You are laughter.
You are hope.

You are a light.
You are a passion.
You are the future.
You are a blessing.
You are a miracle.

You are our miracle.

—
I've never seen him
So full of joy.
Raw, unrestrained
Joy.

Infectious, undeniable
Happiness.
Laughter
In the face of the "impossible."

Tears and nervous laughter,
Unprepared,
Not knowing how to react.

Disbelief.
Cautious optimism.
Irrepressible ecstasy.

We know you're here,
And we couldn't love you more.
You are our baby,
And we love you forever.
To the moon and back,
Our baby you'll always be.

—
From day one,
Everything terrified me.

Is this face wash okay to use?
This soap?
Laundry detergent?
Breakfast?
Coffee?
What about this pillow?

I felt so fragile
And ecstatic
And scared
And important.

I was entrusted with
You.
I was not going to screw it up.
I would not let myself screw it up.

I had so many questions.
My phone died a lot,
Trying to get Google's first, second and third answers on
All
Of
My
Questions.

Is my toothpaste okay for my baby?

—
It was so tempting to start
Making lists,
Reading blogs,
Asking for advice,
Pinning all the things.

I forced myself to not do that just yet.

I was so excited –
But overwhelmingly terrified.
I didn't want to do one thing that might "jinx"
Our miracle baby.

I clung to our first appointment time together,
Imagining what you would look like
On that ultrasound machine screen –
Or if I'd even be able to find you there,
See the progress you had made so far.

Thinking about our first appointment was my sanity,
Because even though I wasn't physically
Making lists,
Reading blogs,
Seeking advice
Or pinning all the things –
My mind was working overtime,
Getting ready for you.

—

After the disbelief and excitement
Of finding out about you,
Our little miracle,
I was worried.

Would I be a good mom?
Would you be proud to have me as a mom?
Would you be disappointed?

I know we're always
Learning,
Adapting,
Growing,
But I felt behind.

Was I prepared?
Being your mom was
Everything
I had prayed for –
I wasn't expecting this
Wave of worry
To overwhelm the excitement.

I pushed away the worry
(Which I'm usually unable to do)
and promised myself – and you –
to be the best mom
I could possibly be.

—
Before I knew about you,
I knew about you.

I had a lightness,
Airiness,
Inexplicable energy
Fluttering around in my body.

I felt like I had
"fragile"
"this way up"
written all over my body.

I felt excited,
But cautious.
Curious,
But scared to take a test.
Hopeful,
But terrified.

—
It was a quiet day, normal day, in the office.
I was content,
Tapping away on the computer,
Organizing spreadsheets and
Storing emails into folders.

I felt something,
And walked into the bathroom.

Something was wrong.

I wasn't sure what, why, or the extent of it, but —
Red —
Something was wrong.

Panicking on the inside,
I quietly walked back into my office,
Grabbed my purse,
And walked out the door.

Driving home I was numb.
My good guy voice was working overtime —
But the rest of me, especially my bad guy voice,
Wasn't having it.
So numbness it was.
No singing, no talking, no thinking.
Numbness.

I got home,
Where I was supposed to feel safe.
But I felt out of place.
Lost.

Something was wrong —
So much red.

—
To me, you already existed.
You were beautiful.
You were joyful, compassionate
And beautiful.

I had so many plans for you —
I could feel you —
I knew how special you were.

You had everything.
You had your whole life ahead of you.
A clean, blank slate.

I will always wonder who you would have become.

—
Complete and utter despair
Flooding through me
Unable to breathe
Choking
Realizing what's happening
But refusing to accept
The inevitable.

Flashing
Through diapers, late nights,
A nursery full of smiling giraffes.
Through laughter, warmth,
Homework, field trips,
A wedding.

Panic,
Because I'm alone.
It's my body, my rejection,
My fault.

We created him,
But
I lost him.

My mind replays
Everything.
What could have gone differently,
What should have gone differently,
What might have created a different outcome.

It's my fault.

—
Each day, I logged on to an app
To check on you.

An app.

How incredible is it that we can
Track your movements,
Your progress,
Your development –
All before you arrive?

I loved learning about you.

Your dad and I would check
On your size,
Your body parts,
What we could expect next.

We were so busy focusing on you,
That we missed what else we might have to face.

—
Numbness swallows me whole.
I can't breathe.
I don't want to – what if that creates more damage?
Panic.
Shock.
Grief.
Numbness overtakes it all.

My mind tries to be the good guy.
Spotting is a thing, yes?
It can be normal.
It is normal.
See that forum there?
That girl had spotting.
That girl bled for a week
And still had her baby.
That girl had a scare
But her doctor said she's fine.
More rest, more water.
You're fine.
It's normal.

My body is the bad guy.
You're really turning to the internet again?
Feel this –
This is not normal.
How about this –
This is not fine.
You really still need more evidence?
Fine, here's more.
Still holding on to that support forum?

—
You had a wonderful support system
Waiting for you.

Your grandparents
Were picking out grandparent names –
"grandma" was off the table.

Your aunt
Bought you the sweetest onesie.

Your siblings
Were preparing and planning
To teach you
How to bark, play, and smuggle treats out to give them.

Your dad
Was over the moon.
He is so strong, thoughtful and determined.
He was ready to
Protect you from the evils of this world,
Train you how to fight for yourself,
Beat you on Xbox
And camp with you under the stars.

Your mom
Had already made you her number one priority.

—
I clung to the online forums for dear life.

I found hope in her story,
Her scare,
Her experience.

Mine could be like them.
Mine was like theirs.
You were still here.
You were fine.
False alarm.
Right?

I needed so desperately to relate to these women,
Who thought something was wrong
But everything turned out fine.

I swallowed the screams of pain that made
My body seize and twist and ache.
I sent them to a soundproof room.
Locked them up,
Threw away the key,
And moved on to page 14 of the forum.

—
I was so ready to be a mom.

I wanted that responsibility.
I wanted that alarm clock.
I wanted that food shower.
I wanted that tantrum.
I wanted you.

—

When we got to the doctor's office,
I felt like a robot.
I was a glass sculpture
Held together with the hope
That you were still here.

I had chosen to listen to my mind,
The good guy.
I just needed the doctor to tell me I was okay,
The good guy was right,
You were still ours.

It took all I had to
Get dressed,
Get in the car,
And walk into that office.

Giant portraits of newborn babies
Smiled back at us
As we waited.

She called us back.
She turned on her computers,
And you were gone –
She talked about you in the past tense,
Her words jumbling like gibberish.

I wanted to scream.
I wanted her to look harder, closer.
I wanted her to get a second opinion.
I wanted her to be your advocate.

You had to be there –
The forums said so,
The good guy said so.
But you weren't there.

—

When we first learned about you,
We made the decision to share
Our miracle with everyone.
I have not and will never regret that.

You are so loved.

You are so loved,
That your family bought you gifts.
A sweet giraffe onesie
That melted my heart
And terrified me
At the same time.

Now
I don't know what to do with the
Sweet giraffe onesie
In the blue box
Marked with happy handwriting.
"Baby"

It took me a year to throw away
My "belly book"
With the five complete pages
And all the unknown, empty pages.

It hurt me to throw it away,
But that's what I needed to do.

I don't know what to do with
The clothes you never got to wear.

—
She was pregnant.
In the office with the baby photos,
The ultrasound technician with the past tense,
And my failure of being a mother –
The nurse in my room was pregnant.

My pregnant nurse
In her purple shirt
Quietly encouraged me,
Assuring me of my situation's normalcy.

One in four.
One in four women
Miscarry.
I'm not alone.
That's what she wants me to know,
But it's not helping.
It only makes me sadder.

I'm a sensitive person,
Trustful to a fault.
I know that my purple pregnant nurse
Was a sweet person
Who only meant to help,
And who was only trying to do her best in such a situation.

But my feedback to this office,
If they had given me a comment card –
Don't assign the purple pregnant nurse
To the glass sculpture
Of a woman who just received confirmation
Of her baby's death.

—
I felt so much shame,
Guilt,
Dirty even.

How could I let harm come to
My baby
Before he was even here?

What kind of mother
Couldn't keep of her baby alive?

I hated telling people about losing you.
I couldn't stand looking in their eyes,
Or reading what they responded with on a text message.

The heaviness was suffocating.
The shame that I had lost you,
Disappointed you,
Failed you –
Was too much.

—
Driving home
After they confirmed
You were gone,
I held your dad's hand.

I held his hand and
Nodded as he tried his best
To comfort me – us – and love.
I nodded as
Tears poured down my face
Like we were running you a bath.
But you weren't there anymore,
And you didn't need a bath –
So why did the water keep falling?

—
The week after we lost you,
Your siblings joined me
In my grief.

They snuggled, slept and cried
With me.

You guys would have loved each other.
They have such kind, gentle souls
And you were a miraculous wonder.

We love you so much.

—
Giraffes are one of my favorite things.
They just make me happy.

Beauty,
Grace,
Poise,
Confidence,
Silly faces,
Awkward,
Gangly.

Whether they're on a card,
In a meme,
The charm on a necklace
Or stuffed with fluff,
Giraffes bring a smile to my face.

They're my favorite –
And I think they were yours, too.

—
I miss you so much,
That sometimes it rips me apart.

I go back through every second
Of our time together,
Trying to figure out what I did wrong.

What I ate,
Touched,
Drank,
Stood near,
Looked at...
That made me lose you.

I miss you all the time
And it terrifies me to think it could happen again.

—
Miscarriage.
Can we talk about that word?
Miscarry.
Mis-carry.

I hate that word.
No wonder we don't talk about it.

It literally implies that the mother
Has failed to carry her child
In the correct way.

And yet they tell us it's not our fault –
When it was our – it was my
Body that rejected my child.
I failed my child.

In the one place where my child
Was supposed to feel
Welcome, warm, safe, protected –
Because God knows that is not this world anymore –
That place failed him.
Rejected him.
My body rejected him.

My body killed him.

—
The doctors,
Your dad,
My family –
Everyone told me to get some rest,
Take some medicine to ease the pain a little.

I nodded,
But inside I was screaming.
Ease the pain a little?

I needed to feel every ounce of this pain –
I deserved this pain.
You were gone,
And the last of you was this pain.

I wasn't about to lose that, too.

——
I talk to myself quite a bit –
Always have.

If I'm in public,
The commentary is usually in my head.
If I'm alone,
The conversation is real, it's verbal.

When you were here,
It was magical.
I wasn't talking to myself anymore.
I was talk to
You.
I was venting to
You.
I was brainstorming with
You.

Our own private party –
Inside jokes,
Bucket lists,
Dreams,
Goals,
Desires,
Laughter.

I miss our talks.

How many of these pieces begin with "I?"

"I" thought this.
"I" feel this.
"I" do this.

Your mother really isn't that vain, that selfish.
At least,
She sure doesn't hope so.

She wishes we could read
Both sides of the conversation.

But we can't.
And truly,
"I" miss you.

—
From the start
We were so excited to
Celebrate you,
Our tiny miracle.

We waited until
We had a blood confirmation
Of the pregnancy.

Then we started calling
Your family members –
Grandparents, aunts, uncles,
Friends.
They were all so happy
And excited to meet you
And get to know you.

Calling (or texting) them later on,
Telling them about losing you –
That was hard.

Hard because you were gone,
Because we couldn't meet you.
Hard because I had failed you.

Even with all the bad news
We had to spread
About losing you –
I'd do it again.
I'm so glad we chose to share our excitement,
Our celebration.

—
Walking into the room
For my first therapy session,
I knew I had picked the right person.
Neutral colors, lots of pillows,
Simple art, lots of windows.
Yes, this was peaceful.
Yes, this felt right.

Then came the talking.

I was there for the fixing part.
I was there to ease my anxieties,
To be able to be around people with children again,
To make it a day without crying,
To not have panic attacks,
To forgive myself.

However –

I underestimated the amount of talking
I would need to do
Before that would happen.
I underestimated the pain that still lingered,
That came up in full force
When I had to do all of this talking.

—

What hurt the most
was losing who you would become.
What you would accomplish.
How you would bless the world.
Where you would grow up, grow old.

My body ached,
But the physical pain was
Nothing
Compared to the pain the world felt
With your loss.

My baby,
You are important.
You are loved.
You are a miracle,
And my baby you'll always be.

—
Triggers are tricky.
One day,
Everything reminds you.
Everything makes you want to scream.
Everything feels like a sharp, twisty knife
In the softest part of your belly.
Everything reminds you of
What you don't have –
What your body rejected –
What you lost.

The next day,
Everything is normal.
It's regular, content, almost boring.
No screaming,
No knives,
No unwanted reminders.
Just life.

Triggers can be funny like that.

—
While you were with us,
I had the most vivid dreams.

I've always had realistic, memorable dreams,
But these were different.

Your dad was there —
And you, our baby.
There was always so much hope, love and laughter.

I never got to see your face —
But you were so beautiful.

You reminded me how
Short life is,
How not to take anything – or anyone – for granted.

Thank you, sweet baby, for the dreams.

You still visit my dreams sometimes.
I'm never expecting it;
You always take me by surprise
And never fail to brighten my day.

I put off therapy for a long time.
I thought I could handle myself.

I'm capable,
I'm independent,
I'm stubborn.
I have trouble with asking for help.

I also felt silly.
I lost our miracle baby, yes.
I hurt every day, yes.

But – what about the friend who lost her child further along?
What about the woman who was still struggling to get pregnant?
What about the acquaintance who gave birth to a sleeping angel?

What was my pain compared to theirs?

I felt silly for feeling hurt.
I felt selfish for thinking my story even compared.

Remind me again why I was comparing stories.

—
Let's take a minute here –
Yes, let's talk for a minute.

Your problem today maybe minute, or
Your problem might be big enough to block the sun.
        Either way, it's valid.

Your biggest obstacle of the week might be that you stubbed your toe, or
It could be that you lost your job.
        Either way, it's valid.

Everyone has a story.
You can't compare apples to oranges,
The beginning of a story to the middle,
Or your idea of success to someone else's.

You have a story,
And it's beautiful.
You are here on this earth and
        You matter.

Instead of comparing yourselves,
I challenge you to lift each other up.
The days will be a whole lot brighter.

Your dad is a good man.
He was, is, and always will be.

He loves you,
And misses you.
He was prepared to be a father.
He would and will be a marvelous father –
And is, every day, to your furry siblings.

He is funny,
Kind,
Smart,
Determined,
Brave,
Strong,
Thoughtful,
Protective,
And stubborn –
Just like your mom,
And probably like you would have been.

Your dad is the type of man
Who will tow a stranger out of a ditch,
Give a homeless person his sweatshirt,
And write me a sappy card because
He knows I need it.

He is a good man –
A great man.
It's important you know who you come from.

—

A lot of my
Actions, choices and thoughts
Used to be guided by,
Haunted by,
And created
Because of what
He/she/they
Would think.
How
He/she/they
Would feel.

Am I really that self-involved?
Do I really think their time is devoted to watching me, judging my actions?

I still struggle with
That voice
Looking out for
Those outside people –
The external advocate
With a different agenda.

I still have insecure, panicky, decision-confused days.

But when I learned
You were here –
I immediately knew I
Shouldn't
Couldn't
And wouldn't be that type of person.

It was time to stand up for you –
And for me.
Thank you for teaching me that.

—
Hearing the pitter-patter
Of sharp nails
And the whooshing
Of happy tails
Clicking on the hardwood floors
Makes my heart sing.

A full house –
People to cook for,
Fuss over,
Clean up after –
Brings me joy.

Conversation, good food, games,
Community.

Having the purpose,
Opportunity,
And blessing
To share food, community and joy
Is one of my love languages.

I long to share that with you.

Sweet baby,
You were my heart's song,
My joy,
My community,
My love language.

—
Over a year later
And I'm sitting in an
Uninterrupted,
Calm
Bubble bath –
Complete with candles and wine.

Every so often,
I lean out of the tub
Listening.
Ready for someone to need me.
Wanting someone to need me.

But you're not here,
And that call doesn't come.

On a good day,
I sigh and imagine
What that call would be like.

On a bad day,
I cry
And relive it all over again.

Either way,
When I hear someone talk about having
"no peace"
"too many interruptions"
"no space"
my heart breaks a little.

I crave that lack of peace and space so desperately.

—
I got a tattoo of a giraffe
On the back of my arm
For me.

It took me a day and a half
To convince myself
I was worth indulging in –
I could get that tattoo.

I put aside what he would think,
What they would assume,
What she might conclude.

My giraffe is a symbol of
Grace,
Strength,
Beauty and most importantly,
Confidence.

Confidence.

At first, I thought it hurt.
And then I remembered you –
And when I lost you.

And it didn't hurt anymore.

—
I'm not sure if you'll have any
Brothers or sisters
In the future.
I do know that if you do,
They'll know about you
And will love you as much as we do.

I think of you every day.

I wonder what you would look like now,
Almost one year old –
So grown up!

I see people post pictures of their children
On social media.
My emotions have changed over time –
From sad to angry to happy.
Numbness fluctuates, too.

Seeing photos of other babies,
Imagining your life with us,
And being inspired by you –
It makes me want to be a better person.

On a lazy, unproductive day,
I wonder what you would think of your mom.

Would you be disappointed?
Annoyed?
Would you use my laziness
As a blueprint for your own choices?

You inspire me, challenge me, motivate me –
Even now.
I want to do that – and more – for you.
I want you to be proud of me.
I want you to be proud of your mom.

Dear Sarah,

I forgive you.

It was not your fault.
You did nothing wrong.
You gave all your love, your hope, your trust,
your emotions and your priorities
To your beautiful child.

You did nothing wrong.

Sarah, you scream "I'm sorry."
You lament, "It's my fault."
Sarah, it's not.
But I forgive you – and release you from
That anger,
That resentment,
That numbness.

Your child was an
Incredible, gorgeous, flawless miracle
Who inspired hope and created happiness
For you and your family.

Your baby –
He was perfect.

You did not kill him.
Your body is not a murderer.
You did nothing wrong.
You are not at fault.

He loves you,
He loves his father,
He loves his sweet, furry siblings.

He would not want this
Numbness
For any of you.

I forgive you.
Your precious baby forgives you.

Your baby he'll always be.

Made in the USA
Middletown, DE
21 August 2021

46601391R00033